The Unhinging of Wings

The Unhinging of Wings

POEMS BY

Margo Button

OOLICHAN BOOKS
LANTZVILLE, BRITISH COLUMBIA, CANADA
1996

Second Printing January 1997
Third Printing June 1997

Canadian Cataloguing in Publication Data

Button, Margo, 1938-
The unhinging of wings

Poems.
ISBN 0-88982-162-3

1. Schizophrenia—Poetry. I. Title.
PS8553.U873U53 1996   C811'54   C96-910588-6
PR9199.3.B88U53 1996

Oolichan Books gratefully acknowledges the support received for its publishing program from the Canada Council's Block Grants program, the British Columbia Ministry of Small Business, Tourism and Culture, and the Department of Canadian Heritage.

Published by
Oolichan Books
P.O. Box 10, Lantzville, B.C.
Canada VOR 2HO

Printed in Canada by
Morriss Printing Company Limited
Victoria, British Columbia

Cover photo and photo of Randall Button by Margo Button.
Photo of Margo Button by Gordon Lafleur.

For Randall, my beloved son

1967-1994

These Poems

read the unwrinkled palms
of your silence while you
shift, fade, vanish.
Leaf prints on a sidewalk
when the leaf has blown away.
These poems, imprecise asides,
I hide from you, presuming
to be the scribe while you
live the agony. I offer them
instead of engravings on granite,
forgotten in a graveyard.

Acknowledgements

Some of the poems in this collection were published in *Canadian Woman's Studies, Prairie Fire, Prism International, Event, Museletter, The Antigonish Review, Contemporary Voices 2, Dalhousie Review, Canadian Writers' Journal, Friends, Portal, Fiddlehead, Dandelion, Canadian Literature, Queen's Quarterly*, and *SCARP* (Australia).

One poem is forthcoming in *Quarry*.

Poems have appeared in the anthologies: *Coastlines 11, Rain Forest, Vintage 94, Vintage 95,* and are forthcoming in *Vintage 96,* and the *1995-1996 Anthology of Magazine Verse and Year book of American Poetry*.

I wish to thank Ron Smith who encouraged and guided me from the start; Millie Tremblay, Leanne Smith, and Sharlya Gold who read the manuscript and offered so many good suggestions; and my husband, Ron, for love and understanding and Earl Grey tea every morning at eleven.

Preface

I'm sitting here tonight on a beautiful Vancouver spring evening, thinking sad thoughts. I'm thinking of a student, a young girl who had just finished her Ph.D. thesis four days ago. Two days ago, she was riding home from the laboratory on her bicycle and a speeding motorcyclist hit her and killed her and himself. That, in turn, is making me think of a day almost 30 years ago when another vibrant young girl student died in front of me because of her defective heart. Two young people dead; dead in the prime of life with their futures and all its promise before them.

Margo Button's son died, too. Not of something comprehensible, although unacceptable, such as a traffic accident or heart disease, but of something we can't understand, the consequence of serious illness, schizophrenia. Death because of schizophrenia did not come suddenly. It was preceded by hallucinations, by hearing voices, by paranoia of a hypersensitive kind. The unhinging that schizophrenia is, is frightening for the affected son or daughter and is bewildering for the parents. And, for most people, for a very long time it can be that no one seems to understand. When they do understand, the treatment seems, often, to be inappropriate or to cause as many problems as the disease itself.

About one percent of the population become schizophrenic. In Canada, that means over 250,000 people. Of those afflicted people, about forty percent attempt to commit suicide, and twenty-five per cent of that group succeed. Margo Button's son succeeded. Another young person cut off in the flower of his youth.

Margo Button has a special talent. She is a poet. Throughout her son's illness with schizophrenia and after his death, she wrote poems. These poems are collected together in *The Unhinging of Wings*. Read them, reflect on their beauty, on their appropriateness, and think about the insight they give into the awful disease that is schizophrenia, and then let Margo Button's contribution to your understanding help you to work for the eradication of this terrible and particularly human disease.

Dr. Michael Smith
(Winner of the Nobel Prize for Chemistry, 1993)

Contents

Part 1 / Glass Cages

Part 2 / Butterfly World

Part 3 / Fractal Landscapes

Randall John Button, 1967-1994

1
Glass Cages

Tell me the truth. How does it end?
Who will untangle their matted hair?
Shine in the dark hole of their sleep?
Though they rattle the bones in their broken brains,
in their thicket of words who will find a way,
discover a path through unmapped terrain?
When will the unpretentious air
fall like rain on the ache of their skin?
What is the price they pay for pain?

Though they go mad they shall be sane.

P.K. Page *Hologram*

Glass Cages

I think of you this morning when a dove
hurtles into the window. Brief image

of himself as other before he crumples
against glass that looks like open sky.

An unhinging of wings. Invisible
shattering. Pearly drift of feathers

across the patio. Two doves flutter
back and forth in constant cortège

while he patiently attends his dying.
His cries, camouflaged so softly.

Chinese Characters

I dream of drowning, clambering to the surface
on rungs that are not there. My head,
pushed down by hands unseen. I awake,
a prisoner, gasping in a sealed hotel room,
knowing I have to return home

where the heart is, home where the ache is.
I long to escape like the friends
whose only son caught fire one night at a gas pump.
They sold their house, quit their jobs, carried
their pain in suitcases all over the world.

But here at the door is my son, come to beg.
He hunkers in bulky Sally Ann coat.
His shaven skull in a knotted scarf,
feet in stinking Chinese slippers with holes. His eyes
burn like those who rave in the streets,

the ones I avoid for fear of recognition.
We go out for breakfast. This wretch,
disguised as my son, and I sip bitter coffee.
Above his head on the wall, black slashes
on fine rice paper:

Mother,
sweeping arms encircling a dot;

Endurance,
sword poised above an open heart.

Blank Years

1

For twenty years I measured time
by you, chronometer of my years,
heartbeat of my days.

But since you've been absent, events
flow together. Shards in molten glass,
streaked with hues of pain.

You surface once in a while, disembodied
voice on a phone. Where, you won't tell.
I stop saying, *I love you*. A life line of caring

doesn't reach that barren ground
where you live. I have no more questions
to ask, no more advice to give.

2

One night, in Vancouver, chained
by umbilical steel, I go off at half tilt
to find you on Skid Row. I inquire

in grimy hotels where drunks piss at the door.
I search the faceless who shoot up
on park benches. I follow

a jaunty walk, a curly head, that dear slight form,
but not you. At open windows, I listen
as I listened at the crib for that tiny breath

that stitched your life to mine.

The Shaman

When I ask why you don't call,
you say there's no need.
I know your thoughts, Mom. I can travel
on the astral plane. I've discovered
the secrets of the universe. Your eyes
are wild with raw light, the certainty
that you are chosen. I want to believe
this is smugness of youth, or a marijuana vision.
But there is jarring in your jumbled words,
a sticky strangeness in the ranting
that frightens even me
who would have followed you to Hell.

The Corkscrew

When he received the phone call
from Medicine Hat, your father flew out
to help you. You'd gone to a police station.
A Nazi and a blonde are trying
to kill me. They've buried
a corkscrew in my head. You showed him
where it pierced your temples from right to left.
You have to believe me, Dad! Dad?
And he, his throat, stoppered with such love and pain
that only a few words trickled out,
Yes, Son, I believe you.

Culpa

> Maybe madness is just an accident. A gun
> that goes off by mistake . . . You aim at the sky
> — and the bullet goes through your brain.
>
> • Timothy Findlay, *The Headhunter*

1

A generation ago, psychiatrists
concocted a brutal blame,
sanctified it with a medical term:

schizophrenogenia.
Mothers drive children mad.
Like the goddess Kali, they create
and they destroy.

> I know a mother with three sons,
> two schizophrenic. The third
> left home, rejected her
> for destroying the other two.

2

At first, his father and I
blame each other for the way
our son turns out. Then, I blame myself.
Mother used to say, *You'll see*

what suffering is when you have your own.
Then, I blame marijuana and
the girlfriend who supplies him.
Maybe, he just needs to grow up.

When he screams at the corkscrew
splitting his skull, doctors diagnose
drug-induced schizophrenia.
Maybe, if he stops the drugs.

3

Now I know there is no one to blame,
but that impassive god
who shoots stray bullets
through the brain.

Lord Randall
(variation on a folk song)

"O where hae ye been, Lord Randall, my son?
O where hae ye been, my handsome young man?"
"I hae been to Four Corners; mother, make my bed soon,
For I'm weary wi' riding, and fain wald lie down."

"What did you there, Lord Randall, my son?
What did you there, my handsome young man?"
"I questioned the shamans, mother; make my bed soon,
For I'm weary wi' talking, and fain wald lie down."

"What wisdom did you learn, Lord Randall, my son?
What wisdom did you learn, my handsome young man?"
"That my mind is away; mother, make my bed soon,
For I'm weary wi' searching, and fain wald lie down."

"What burns in your eyes, Lord Randall my son?
What burns in your eyes, my handsome young man?"
"The spectres that haunt, mother; make my bed soon,
For I'm weary wi' seeing and fain wald lie down."

"What gat ye so thin, Lord Randall my son?
What gat ye so thin, my handsome young man?"
"The voices that taunt, mother; make my bed soon,
For I am weary wi' listening, and fain wald lie down."

"I fear ye are ailing, Lord Randall my son!
I fear ye are ailing, my handsome young man!"
"I swear it's the truth, mother; make my bed soon,
For I am sick at the heart and fain wald lie down."

New Son

I search the blur for the son I knew,
but you elude me like the smoke
you huddle over. You are thin and
bent, a husk from an ear of sweet corn,
discard after the harvest, fodder during
five dread years in the streets. Your arms

hang like folded wings as you ghost
along the walk. Your feet shuffle, avoid
the crunching leaves. Your embrace feels
tremulous. *It's so good to be home,* you say,
as you go through the motion of smiling.
Your eyes lower like blinds to shut out
the light of others, or pierce like a laser,

too bright. *You look peaceful, Mom,* you say,
and I am glad you no longer know me,
you who knew me so well. I forget
the questions I came with, take your
limp hand in mine, stroke the elegant fingers,
get to know you. Wh*at are you thinking?*
Nothing, you say, unashamed.

Reunion

Your grandfather is there
the day you come home. We've just heard
the verdict. My son my dear my only,
you are schizophrenic.

You sit among us, vacant, your body
shrunken like an empty laundry bag.
Prodigal son, you return to inhabit
landscapes you never share, talk
to demons you never meet,
serve in the army of devil's children.

You wear Grandpa's old sneakers
because you've lost your own.
Your fingers are long and graceful
like his. But he pretends you are
air, as he sits across the room,
chats about the evening news.

It's weeks since he called. He recites
excuses: *I'm a bit lazy.*
I'm getting too old for emotions.
Finally, I confront him, *It seems*
you don't care. He looks at me
sharply, through tears,
How can you say such a thing?

The Laundering

He is with us for Christmas, the first time
in years. A derelict with a shopping bag
of dirty clothes. His feet are rank
like water from a vase of wilted flowers.

I send him to bathe and change his clothes.
Too old for orders, he obeys. We talk about
the two dollar sneakers he bought at Sally Ann,
why he loses shoes, forgets to change socks.

The new Nikes I bought, he refuses
to wear. The insteps have plastic triangles.
He's afraid he'll slide out of them into
sticky shadows on city streets. *Covering the exits*

with marker pen doesn't help, he says. Alone,
in the laundry room, I slip to my knees, hold
lemon warmth to my face. Fold love
with tears into his clean socks and shirts.

Christmas Letter

Greetings again from all those friends
with successful sons. *Our Richard*
has just finished medical school. He's married now.
We're going to be grandparents in the spring.
And how is your son?

Maybe for once I'll leave the saccharine scenes
unopened: perky little dogs with red bows
performing for the camera. My friends won't know
I passed up the *petits fours* messages.
Cocktail tidbits gag me now. I don't want
to drink a toast; ice cubes reveal too much.

I could send a computer letter, personalized
in the first and last lines, a hundred copies
of a sugar-coated life. Or I could tell the truth.

Dear Friends:

1992 was a good year. Our son left Skid Row.
He committed himself to a psychiatric ward.
He is twenty-five years old.
No interests, no job, no friends.
Each day he sits, smokes, eats, sleeps,
                sits, smokes, eats, sleeps.

This is my joy: he survived.
Hi, Mom, he calls, softly, on the phone, wonders
if he's still wanted after all that has passed.
His body quakes with the medicine. Without it,
he disappears into Star War worlds of his own.

Home for the holiday, he touches cool onyx to cheek.
I recall when life was green and gold
like the ashtray I give him. Long fingers
reach out to take my hands in his.
I love you Darling. Me too, he says.
Merry Christmas.

Gifts

Branches of big firs swoop
in the southeasterlies as we gather
round the Christmas tree. Home at last,
he hugs his thin body in the warmth of the fireplace,
the flames of our love. There is a new
flannel shirt and blue housecoat, a Swiss army knife
from his sister. He examines
the screwdiver, scissors, corkscrew.
Strokes each shiny blade
gingerly, as if it were a woman he loved.

He remembers other knives of fine steel,
sticks he whittled when he was a kid, the face
he carved on the knob of a cane,
the slingshot his dad made. He wore it
around his neck all one summer,
hunting squirrels in the valley.

Suddenly, he wakes as if from a dream.
Wait, he says, running off to his room,
and returning with an open box of
Ram Champa, his only treasure.
The best incense there is, he smiles,
laying it on the table for all of us.

Three weeks later, the knife is gone.
Maybe she's mad at me; maybe she took it back.

With No Explanation

1

One winter day at the lake when
you were small, you went cross country
skiing with your dog. Night came,
and you didn't return. We imagined
you'd broken a leg and lay freezing
in the forest, crying out for us
as we called your name, but we heard
only the crunch of boots along that icy road.
I thought of Hansel, live kindling for a
witch's supper. Fear makes storytellers
of us all. But you returned, red cheeks aglow,
puzzled why we hugged you so hard
for rounding up the errant dog.

2

Now, you recall this memory, as if
it were someone else's story; you are
like the clothes you lose track of. You
do not even know you're gone. Oh Randall!
No use to shout and wail. Cries do not reach
the limbic shores where you float
like a graceful loon whose cries

pierced our summer nights so long ago.
One white morning, you awoke to find
your black feathers rooted in the lake's early freeze.
Your friends had fled. Across the gelid expanse,
I answer your haunting call.
Here I am. Look at me. Talk to me.

Odysseus

Curls fall in cascades, child-like
on his forehead. He could be any young man
having lunch at the pub with his friends,
but eyes betray. Blue pinpoints
skewer the menu glinting in the sun,
their focus too long, too intent.

Graceful fingers reach out. Carefully, surely,
he picks up some   thing
and puts it in his pocket; then,
does it again. I dare not ask
what he sees in these motes of sunshine
passing through his empty hand. I cannot
hurt him in front of witnesses.

I put the menu aside, stifle the shout,
Come back. Come back
from that other world, and tell me the tales
of your travels: the sirens who lure you
to jagged shoals, the cyclops you battle,
the treasures you see in the golden sun.

Schizophrenic

1

He plays *The Grateful Dead* on high
at 5:00 o'clock in the morning,
the door open wide. The manager
finds him cowering in the closet,
arms wrapped stiffly around his thin body
like linen strips on a burn victim. White
ointment highlights the fear on his face.
Looks like toothpaste, the neighbour says.
A cigarette burns a hole in the rug.

Next day, he puts his shoes in the
oven to dry, and goes out for smokes.

2

After the fire, he disappears; I go in
to pick up his things. Scattered
on the rug are slices of toast
from the toaster he put in the fridge.
Nickels and dimes rattle in the crisper.
Foreign Devils Have Light Eyes
lies in the freezer beside malachite
beads that have come unstrung.

Under the sink, *Rats and Gargoyles*
is stashed with the phone he never
answered and the bonsai he begged me
to buy. Dead needles prick my fingers.
A dessicated fish without a tail
curls in the cupboard. Cassettes unwind
among moldy dishes. Tuna tins

of butts and empty lighters tally his hours.
On the floor, shirts and socks, stained
and stiff like cast-off skins, wait for him
to crawl back in. On the medicine shelf,
a ceramic orca whale lies belly up
beside a neat stack of pennies,
a trace of the order he once knew.

The Kris

The kris was from Bali. We bought it
the year after the slaughter when families
fractured, and old debts were settled
under political guise. The blade was a sliver

of meteorite with wave-like edges
to facilitate entry, and long, deep grooves
to drain the blood. The hilt was an ebony lion
with ruby eyes. They say a kris has a history;

to buy one second-hand is bad karma.
Like a grizzly, it acquires a taste for human flesh.
On his bedroom wall it hung beside
two samurai swords. One day they were gone,

pawned in Skid Row for a meal. As he vanished,
so did his treasures. Later, I came upon the blade
stashed in the back of a cupboard, a steel stub
where the lion had been.

Visit to the Doctor

In the middle of the waiting room
he stands, carved in ivory
like a Chinese sage. Black circles
under his eyes drag his gaze to the floor.
Legs and arms are irrelevant
to a pillar of salt
who looks back and remembers, but cannot
move on, 'though he breaks no command.
His is absorbed by the chatter of termites
that burrow dead ends, endlessly in his mind;
by ranting faces that leap, then twist away.
And my heart is bursting, sprouting
red flowers of love, willing him to lift his eyes,
answer the doctor's questions.

Who Has Lost Everything

The madman is not the man who has lost his reason.
The madman is the man who has lost everything
except his reason.

•G.K.Chesterton

1

In high school, he learned to write Mandarin.
Each night, curly head bowed, intent,
he mixed water in the inkstone
until it was soupy black. With bamboo brush

poised just so above the rice paper,
he wrote the character over and over
in each small square. Like a child
learning his first words, he was

delighted at the precision of naming,
the resonance of meaning.
Crisis is composed of two characters:
danger and opportunity.

2

But hidden chaos lurked in his brain. A beast,
that was there from the start, fed on him,
jumbled the languages he learned.
It twisted his mother tongue

into a labyrinth where he lost the thread.
Familiar words became tricksters
who lay in wait with strobe light snares
and dark inkblots. Yet he yearned

to read, to understand the mysteries
he glimpsed, the astral travels he took
when he thought he was a shaman
who talked to us in our dreams.

The Silence

> I heard all things in the heavens and in earth.
> I heard many things in hell. How, then, am I mad?
> •Edgar Allen Poe

My son.

I think of chalk marks on a city street,
the anonymous outline of a victim,
memory of a screech, a thud.

I think of Pompeian ashes, of bodies
that become empty spaces. Archaeologists
fill their contorted forms with plaster,
so we know the look of suffocation,
the guise of stifled screams.

I think of the Iceman trapped in the Alps
during a sudden storm, bony orifices
stopped up by centuries of snow.

I would probe your frozen mask, my son.
I would listen in the Tower of Babel
behind your silent walls.
I would hear the metallic curses
from the corner of the room. Words
with a stuck life of their own
that gum up all your thoughts.
Angelic choirs that sing
in the convoluted circuits of your mind.
I would know who you are.

The Unhinged

People say they have a screw
loose, their brain like a barn door
hanging off its hinges, swinging in the wind,
and no matter how they shut it, the fit
is not right, and the brain pours out

like a dead soldier's intestines that
will not stuff back in. They are
edible food: crackers, bananas,
flakey, nutty as fruitcake, barmy as a crumpet.

Quickly consumed and starving
on the streets. They say they're off their rocker,
doolally, off their trolley, haywire, short-
circuited and stopped in the middle of the road —
the conductor out to lunch while they

are round the bend — there but not there,
like peek-a-boo games with babies.
They call them cuckoos, daft birds
with goofy calls who abandon their eggs
in the nests of others. They say

they are mad as March hares, crackpots
gibbering under a stove-pipe hat
in a world that shrinks, expands, invites
slides into mirrors, walks on moonbeams.
They call them addle-pated, their thoughts

scrambled like goose eggs
into a swirl of stunted wings. They say
they are thimble-witted, their wits
the size of a thumb, their armour
a thimble.

When I Loved You Young

I love you in such a different way
from when I loved you young.
This love is cloth of gold I drape
on your bowed head, around
your stooped shoulders, a mantle
that honours your will to learn

when you can barely read or carry on
a conversation. I wait for an answer.
A muscle twitches in your cheek.
You incline your head as if
words were blows. This love
endures, esteeming endurance

while larvae eat away the fabric
of your mind. So little is left that delights:
a double cappuccino, a new shirt
you rush to put on, fumbling the buttons.
Oh, that love were a magic cape
that could whisk you back to a promised land.

Family Tree

1

In 1808 Caleb Bartlett arrives
in Waweig New Brunswick
His wife Molly bears Caleb and Leonard
whose wife Anna
bears Moses and Jesse and John

On Jan 25, 1821 Anna loses ten-year-old Moses
On Jan 26   twenty-year-old John
She has another son the same year
and names him John

whose wife Susannah bears
Ada and Seth and Angilette
Adith who dies at three
Persha who dies at twenty-four in childbirth
Edward Hitchings who marries

Fannie my great-grandmother
whose sixteen-year-old daughter
Fannie May dies
of an appendectomy performed at home

Helen my grandmother loses
Roger her son of twenty-six
when he plunges over a cliff in a car
I know the forever-young Mountie
from the photograph that takes his place
A nephew takes his name

You women churn out babies every year
to fill the God-forsaken void
but loss is the daily bread you bake

2

In the summer of '92   I return to the family home
Stumps remain of the four old elms
that framed the white farmhouse   Here
in the barnyard I made mud pies with pee
when I was two   Sweet grasses buzz and blow
in the sun where Dad ran with his brothers
and sister Anna   the aunt I resemble

Only Dad and his brother remain
of Bartlett's whose photos once covered the wall
We eat lobster sandwiches at Grandpa's oak table
Uncle talks about the folks down the road
who had a son an only son   They locked him
in the barn when he had a crazy spell

I imagine fists pounding splintery wood
until they bled in the black where the voices were
Fists in my chest   *My son Randall John*
I tell them   *is mentally ill*
The cause is genetic   The prognosis is not good
I want to add *I regret I cannot replace him*
but I will not let him disappear

Dad twists his mouth and scowls at the sideboard
He wishes I hadn't brought it up   Uncle studies
the crusts on his plate   This family of men know
only the touch   of handshakes   They talk easily
about the price of shingles at the sawmill or the deer
whose soft white bellies they slit in the fall   Pain
they pour down their gullets and piss out in the drain

A Thing of Beauty

1

Three stories up, sturdy men wedge and nail
a scaffold across an open tower.
Rough hands raise a cupola
in the blazing sun. A white breast
pointed at heaven and glistening with tints
of jungle and sky. The nipple, a graceful spire.

Mucha pólvora, I say to the foreman.
He smiles, and fakes a gunshot wound
at his temple. No, that's not the word.
Mucho polvo , he corrects,
indicating the dust his men
track through the house.

Oil tins of wet cement carve their shoulders
as they trudge on last week's news
laid out on the stairs. A headline catches my eye:
Young Canadian, murdered in Cabo.
I picture a long distance call,
a body shipped home in a box.

2

Last night, someone phoned to say
that my son jumped from a third floor window.
I heard whispers all over the room,
he told the police. *I thought I could walk
on a beam of light.* He smashed
his pelvis, elbow, heel. The right foot

was pulverized. *I cannot glue dust to dust,*
the doctor says. I picture my son
dancing on drops of bright neon rain,
flying like a bird with hollow bones.
That perfect small body I once carried,
shattered on cement.

Freedom

After a month you check yourself out of hospital,
hobble away on two broken feet.
You buy a cane and sneakers
from the Sally Ann. You squeeze your swollen feet
inside, laces undone. You believe
you can heal yourself with the quartz crystal
in your pocket. Your hair is matted
like moss in the rain forest. Your face
is a compass pointing north to the islands,
to salt spray and pungent fir, to a moon-pocked beach
where you curl up uncovered
one windy night in March. An injured animal,
at home in the lap of the sea.

Suits of Woe

Worn-out garments
Are shed by the body.
Worn-out bodies
Are shed by the dweller.
Within the body
New bodies are donned
By the dweller, like garments.
  • *Bhagavad-Gita*

When his words disappeared, I came to know him
by his clothes. Snakeskins he shed,
chrysalises from which he never
emerged, the measure of his descent
into darker worlds. Clothes became his enemies,
full of vermin and troubling spirits.
He burned them, lost them, gave them away.
He didn't mean to. I saw the hurt
in his eyes, the refusal to be chastised.

Among his clothes, I found a T shirt
with two loons hugging and having the time
of their lives. Below them was written:
"Hug me. I'm a Loony."

Clothes were dreams he purchased
at the Sally Ann. The young man about town
in bright silk shirt, leather jacket, collar turned up
for a week or two. But after a while,
any cast-off would do. Any brand
covers up the remnant of a man.

He was like a monk in sackcloth, a member
of a silent order dressed in black or grey,
shirts with no designs, no names. He wore
hoods like a hangman to hide his face. His body
was a relic he lost touch with, skin and bone
in a hairshirt, made of twisted rope
and knots and nails of nightmares.

When he couldn't suffer any more, he jumped
into the neon night. The doctors
sewed him up, then took away his clothes,
tried to keep him prisoner
long enough to mend. But he walked out the door,
an emperor on two broken feet.

Narcissus Poeticus

Christmas poinsettias have not dropped
their blood petals when the first daffodils
quiver in my garden—brave lilies of Lent
with sunny faces and long necks. They are vigilant
of southerlies that fell them like gentle trees,
and drag their yellow skirts through the soil.

In the dead fir, the starling crushes
her rustling feathers into a hole, warms
her hushed eggs below the eagle's perch.
On the rocky shore, the cormorant spreads
his heavy wings to dry, a black crucifix
in the sun. I gaze at the fickle sea,
wonder at sadness in the heart of spring.

2
Butterfly World

I would like to fling my voice out like a cloth
over the fragments of your death, and keep
pulling at it until it is torn to pieces,
and all my words would have to walk around
shivering, in the tatters of that voice;
if lament were enough. . .

Rainier Maria Rilke   *Requiem*

Red Shoe Polish

One day when you were two,
you found some red shoe polish.

While I was cooking dinner,
you put on mushy carmine gloves,

streaked your blond curls
scarlet, painted the sofa

in an orgy of crimson delight.
When I saw you I screamed.

I thought you were bleeding
to death, as I did this morning

when I found you on the steps
leading down to the sea.

Samurai

On the black altar table, you laid
your silver chain, an offering
in front of two Japanese dolls
dressed in stiff gold and orange brocade.
Porcelain faces, impassive black eyes
like those of the girls you once caressed.
In the centre of the bed, you placed
a rose quartz — a gentle good-bye,
a wordless embrace.

You sat on the steps leading
down to the sea. On the steps where
chimes play fleeting wind melodies, and
humming-birds bicker over sweet water,
dyed red. Beside the azalea that
cracked last winter from its burden of snow,
you faced east to stunted fir and dark mountains,
and you plunged the knife
again and again into your chest.

On the Steps Leading Down

1

I found you in the morning, face up, spellbound
by unravelling clouds.
Randall? Randall? Then I saw
hilt of knife, scarlet chest
thrust upward, white dog at your feet.
Still, all still.
Lying on the steps in bright spring sun,
young Adonis gored, blood like scarlet anemones
strewn across the fields — a pool beside you
of melted red petals.
Your head wrenched back, stone eyes
half vanished, grey lips agape in grey face.
An intruder. There on the steps
leading down to the sea, to the sea, this horror —
Oh Randall, my beloved son.

2

Now, I scatter chrysanthemums
and narcissus on the spot. And when
they wilt, I scatter more and more

where your dear body forever lies, where
no flowers will ever spring,
on the steps leading down to the sea.

Snowball

He lay at your feet, an afterthought
flung on the stairs. One stab wound
in his fluffy white fur. *Snowball,*
who barked at lions on tv, then searched for them
behind the set; who flounced lop-sided
up hill and away, deaf to his name;
who careened off the cliff, chasing seagulls.

A pharoah, you dragged him
unwilling to the tomb. Did you think
his howl at that dark hour would undo
your dying? Was his the little body
you practiced on to get the knife thrust right?
Did you want a warm embrace
in the Valley of the Dead?

Passim

I look for you everywhere — in the whisk
of heavy wings that startle from the fir —
dry drop of cones — splayed footprints on white sand.
A Canada goose, who arrived the day after
the funeral, lingers on the lawn, alone
while all the others are mating. Gulls skreel
behind the shrimp boat on a sleek sea.
Pink feet pleat under as they hang-
glide into wind — trifled with by the invisible.
In the twisted fir, one crow rattles sorrow.
The chimes I silenced above the steps
where you died, peal out today for you.

At the Funeral Home

I held hands with my son today,
and I was not afraid. His fingers
were the colour of ivory. They moved
when I moved them, but with no music
of their own. Their grasp was flimsy
like Indian pipes on the rain forest floor.
Wan flowers need no sun. I hungered
to embrace his slight frame, dressed

in graduation suit. I wept
for the broken elbow and pelvis, pulverized feet,
all the old wounds hidden under the lid.
For the brave chest, twice pierced.
I longed to take him home where I might
gaze my fill. I would have soon tired of
powdered cheeks and cold kisses.

Queen of the Night

This ungainly plant projects
in all directions, thrusts
against windows, seeking exits.
One warm day, resigned
to confinement, it erupts
a long green umbilicus
on the side of a leaf.
Thick veins throb, nourish
the bud at its tip. One night,
the pregnant pod bursts
in a white blaze of petals — a bride
in lace and satin and pearls.
At times, a flurry of brides
who honey the air with urgency
as if to say, *Wake,*
this is our wedding night.
Come celebrate with us,
for we must die at dawn.

Butterfly World

The day before you died, we visited
the greenhouse where pupae hang
suspended in glass cases for everyone to see.
Crumpled mummies hide perfection
until one day, damp wings unfold.
Giant Owls emerge with blind eyes
on their wings, brush past us
like apple blossoms in April winds.
They flutter about for a week or two,
seeking the sun beneath a plastic roof.
Briefly you looked, then collapsed
on a bench by the door, your broken feet
pinned to the floor — a specimen
with atropied wings.

Communion

Cherry petals rain below the trees.
Confetti showers at the wedding

of spring. They gather in the shape
of April breezes to dance. Pink

butterflies tumbling on wing tips
across the walk. Paper-thin tongues

caressing the grass, pressing along
edges in a moist *potpourri* of skin.

It is sacrilege to tread when they anoint
with such a gentle laying-on of hands.

The Parting Gift

I knew
each time I walked into hospital,
and found you in the dark, hiding under the sheets.
Once you looked me square in the eye,
branded me for a life time.
I've got to get out of here; they're stealing my soul.

I knew
a week before you died, when I saw you laid out
in the dentist's chair, your teeth bared
in a voiceless snarl, gums bleeding.
White powder dusted your forehead and curls;
white rubber fingers wormed in and out
of your mouth. I knew you didn't want to be here.

I knew
the last day when we walked in the woods.
I led you to the edge of the cliff. *Look
at the candles on the firs. Listen
to the run-off in the canyon.* The child in me
was enticing you to attend to these joys.

I knew
on the way home when I saw Death
playing in the light on your face. I reached out,
held your long fingers in mine.
We were always holding hands, you and I,
and walking arm in arm.

Rose Quartz

1

Two weeks ago, I picked you up
at the hospital to go for a drive.
Mom, I have to buy a rose quartz
I saw in a store on Tenth. Please,
it won't take long. I chuckled,
What's it going to do for you?
Don't laugh, you said
as you hung the heavy charm
in a rainbow pouch around your neck.

2

The morning you died, I found
the rose quartz in the centre
of the bed. Cold stone in the cold
print of your body. Rainbow pouch
discarded on the floor. There were
no other messages.

3

Now at night, caged by flashbacks,
I caress my cheeks with this rock,
as you must have done — solitary prisoner,
eyeing your way in the dark. I push

sharpness into my chest, clench
hardness in my left hand.
The quartz becomes warm, alive —
a chubby hand in mine when you were two.
Love erupts, releases
for a moment. I hear your gentle voice,
Take it easy, Mom. I'm here.

Whales

Under a snow sky, the orca lies
stranded in shallows, waiting for

a tide that never rises. His mother
warbles her love from afar, long after

there is no reply. She bellows when
the polar bear minces the flesh,

once hers. She cannot staunch the
bloody winds that howl in the crevices

of her heart. There are only circles
to carve around and round the bay.

At last, she turns reluctantly to sea,
a lone shard of ice in pellucid waters.

A Man's Grief

After the funeral, he dismantles
the sunroom, and builds a new deck
sealed with tar to keep out winter rains.
He buries himself in *Homes and Gardens*,
shifting angles and shapes. All I want
is a corner to plant my pain. I think of
quitting this house, desecrated now,
grief running down its walls.
With a screeching saw, he removes
the railings, pares them like an apple, and
lets the peeling fall away until
the core of home is revealed, and reveals
the rose garden and firs laden with cones.
Along the decks, he builds a bench, and
paints it blue-black, like a bruise, an armband
wrapped around the house, and the house,
he re-paints, even the blood-soaked steps, the steps
where our dead son has lain, his face
the pallour of grey, and now the house grey too.

First Teddy Bear

Every night I hug him in the cavern
of my belly, plush den you once inhabited,

kicking my body out of shape
until I let you go. Bear's willing arms

encircle my chest, velvet head nuzzles
under my chin. Plastic eyes, stitched nose

with no sweet breath to listen for.
Yet he comforts — a wooden plank

the beluga nudges up and down the river
after her calf has died.

Spring's End

my flesh unfolds no more
once the huge luxury of eggs
I harboured   were

thousands of clematis buds
flawless   chaste pincers
pink and white pledges

that draped languidly
along the fence in spring
wavered on crinkly edges
in summer

they are spent petals now
grey skin melting
into the garden walk
the plant   dismembered

once
a silent hand unhinged
and opened wide my hips

the seed flowered
into perfect bloom
once

The Korean Chest

I am drawn here, not seeking pain,
but enticing you into being
again and again, singeing myself
with memories gathered in a chest, keepsakes
of you behind teak doors.

On top, a brass Buddha stares
from mother-of-pearl eyes — a stone and a chain
in its palm. I open drawers, fondle
a felt heart — *Happy Valintien's Day, Mom and Dad.*
Tiny wrinkled shoes, clippings of hair, a baby's ring
that fits inside the man's. Your life
reduced to the absurd, a few sundries:
empty key ring, wallet, lighter.
Your life telescoped between congratulations
and condolences: *No words can express* . . .

Letters in your cramped handwriting
from Ponoka Mental Hospital
the time you thought a corkscrew
was piercing your skull. *The psyche
is a merry-go-round. Guess you heard
someone attacked mine in my sleep. Don't worry.
Your son is a survivor.* Empty words,
This chest is void.
I must seek you elsewhere.

Hair

In the 19th century jewelers made keepsake
ornaments from the hair of the dead, knotting
long single hairs into arabesqued roses,
initials, birds, butterflies.

> • A. Proulx, *The Shipping News*

When you were a child, your hair glowed
a golden Afro in the sun. Curls
tumbled down your forehead — spicy
wood shavings I buried my kisses in
when our breaths were one.

....

At twenty, you returned home
from Mexico, a half-crazed look
on your face, filthy hair in dreadlocks.

You burned your clothes, rinsed
your hair in formaldehyde
to kill imaginary
vermin that were driving you mad.

....

When your tangled hair reached
your shoulders I took you for a haircut.
Cut, I said to the barber, *Cut*

some more. You protested,
Only an inch, as if you were being
swept away in scattered clippings,
and parts of you would never grow again.

....

In a wheelchair after the accident,
you allowed me once to wash your hair.
I held my breath, afraid
you'd change your mind. It cost you
to be so close, your sense of space
meshed and blurred. And I, devoted
like Mary anointing Jesus' feet with nard
before she dried them with her hair.

....

Now you are dead, I cling
to a few dark strands the undertaker snipped off.
But for the ashes, all that is left
of you, sealed in an envelope.
Oh, that I had gathered those other curls,
woven you into a butterfly.

As I Sit Here, Blind

God is a vivisectionist.

-C.S. Lewis

A screech owl, with the soundless flight
of a moth, strikes like the distant
whip of his call. I hear him tonight
in the woods, among the voices spilling
out of the dark as I sit here, blind.
His eyes are beacons swivelling
in the shadows for victims. And oh,
the ecstasy when he plunges his claws, the delicious
fish-hooking, firking under fur and skin for morsels.
Little tufts of devil's horns on his ears
flick with delight when the meal is done.
Mottled plumes settle
into a perfect disk around his face
while tiny bones churn in his gut.

Nakusp Hot Springs

Long-tongued cypresses lick
the Kootenay winds. Vulture trees
keep company with the dead. I lie
in turquoise pools that fume up
from the nether world. My burning
body floats. Feet detached, bloated
like his, broken before he died.
My veins are swollen green. My limbs,
someone else's, caged by shifting
rainbows. I am reduced to bits
of bone scattered among the trees.

Dark of the Moon

I swim blindly against the undercurrent
of dream. A lingering after-taste
denies the lover beside me. I touch
the cradle of stomach, inhale sweet night

under rain-sprinkled roofs, trail
my comforter in chiaroscuro rooms,
cushion at last against the sofa's
sturdy back. Through the window,

the harbour beacon flashes a heartbeat
every third time. A green light tints
the Chinese scroll on the wall. Mountains
recede in layers of black ink. Fog

hugs their jagged edges — fog created
by the absence of ink. On the lake,
tiny fishermen in sampans — brushed in
with a few strokes. An afterthought.

3
Fractal Landscapes

I coined fractal from the Latin adjective fractus.
The corresponding Latin verb frangere means
"to break": to create irregular fragments.

Benoit Mandelbrot

. . . and then in the startled space which a youth as lovely as a god
had suddenly left forever, the Void felt for the first time
that harmony which now enraptures and comforts and helps us.

Rainier Maria Rilke   *Duino Elegies*

Fractal Landscapes

If you like fractals it is because you are
made of them. If you can't stand fractals,
it's because you can't stand yourself. It happens.
•John Briggs, *The Patterns of Chaos*

Wrinkles all over my face. These faults
in the earth, furrows in the field.
Forks of lightning. Fractures in ice
and pink marble. Bare branching trees when red leaves
have shrivelled. Fingerprints of chaos
cannot be stripped down, cleaned off, studied
under glass. I am a riverbed
eroding into the sea. I am blades
of bruised clouds after a storm. I am
mountains folding and buckling and reborn.

The Afghan

Willed to me as the eldest,
this *potpourri* of old bits of yarn

crocheted into a black web.
A loosening patchwork now,

broken in places. I wrap
the shawl around my shoulders.

A child again, I push through
holes, collect loops on my fingers,

in and out like her hook, weaving
comfort out of air. I tell her of his death.

Mom, in my house, there will be
no prodigal son, no coat of many colours.

My Father's Comfort

Remember, we come of strong stock, he says
in a tremulous voice. His big hand
clenches my arm; his flint eyes blaze
a message. He never comes this close.

I know he's rehearsed, condensed
the speech, weighed each word against the tears
he refuses to shed. His mouth
is skintight across yellow teeth,
worn from the gnawing of eighty years.

I see a giant soup of family
boiling on the hearth. Meat falls away
clean from generations of bones.
Marrow is sucked out. Genes, distilled
like spirits, until an essence remains.
He and I.

A Requiem of Birds

In my bedroom under the roof's resounding
caul, I am a night owl locked in a barn,
swooping among rafters, straining for voices
on the other side.

               A smattering of starlings
fingers the shakes. Then, a syncopated flock,
like the brief pelting of summer showers,
abruptly stops.

               Dead branches crack
and land. Clams clatter to their death,
skewered by seagulls who tread above me
with heavy step.

               A quavering screech.
I know the parted beak with glistening hair,
the eagle's amber eyes. There is a great
mewling and shrieking —

               a requiem of birds.
At daybreak, white feathers petal the lawn.
On the Douglas fir, within reach,
dangles a small skeleton

               with cruciform wings.

On the Skeleton Coast
(after photos by Freeman Patterson)

On the sand dunes beside the sea,
there is a lone house where someone
once lived. Windows gape like mouths
of those asleep or dead

who have nothing to hide; yet,
looking seems an invasion.
Winds have scoured the boards,
scored them in waves like the shore.

Fog has come and gone, peeled away plaster
until a heart of bricks remains.
There are no soft corners to curl up in.
No flowers, no song, only sand

that forces doors ajar, and scoops
against walls like snow against fences.
Sand straggled with sun
under slats of an unadorned sky.

The Butcher Block

Each knife has a slit where it rests, sharp edge up,
ready for use. Paring knife, fillet, bread knife, cleaver,
but the carving knife which hangs behind my eyes, the carving knife
that was your intimate, the carving knife has disappeared.
I see you, entranced, that night as you prepare.

You test the knife on the cutting board, run your finger
along the blade that shines like a saviour. You press the tip
like a dreadful gift against the soft body that wants no pact
with obscene agents. You knew your knives. Not long ago,
you transformed the grainy souls of wood. You carved a flute,

but abandoned it before we heard the song. You carved an old man
on a walking stick, but it fell in the firepit and burned. One day
in the kitchen, I took the paring knife to cut an apple open.
You flinched as if the sweet wet flesh were your own. Ah!
It was not me you feared, but the beloved face of your own longing.

The Embrace

Bloodless lips, blood-soaked shirt, glass eyes
track me day and night. I am chained
to Death. My son raises the dagger, and it is me.
I know his terror, determination, ecstasy.

My breast rises to meet the thrust, rehearses
the slicing of flesh, the resisting scrape
of knife past bone. Once. Twice.
The slow drenching release.

I shove away the searing image that brands me
like a chattel. In my mind's eye, I cover it
with the green sheet they used that morning when
we were all seduced by the stranger in our midst.

I try to recall his last shy embrace.
Thanks for a lovely day, Mom. But the corpse
slimes back, beckons me to sit beside it,
to close its staring blue eyes and slack mouth,
to wash away its blood.

So I gather it, heavy, in my arms.
So I hold it, broken, to my breast.

A Relief of Roses

1

White rosebuds reveal
a blush of yellow
as they uncrumple.
A confusion
before opening wide,

as if the pattern were
suddenly forgotten,
the way lost. Yet, roses
open according to plan.
Bloom. Die.

Each morning, I remove
their bowed heads. Reluctantly,
discard their bruised skin
as I try to get used
to their dying.

2

One night I dream of relief.
A luxuriance
of white roses swirl and uncoil.
Hot nebulae
in the Milky Way.

Fantasy Coffin

In Ghana they carve wooden coffins
for the dead. A farmer is buried
in a bulbous green onion. A mechanic,
in a Yamaha 40. A fisherman,
in a snapper, lined with pink satin.

For you, I'd have ordered a black Triumph
with red leather seats, the car of your dreams,
made of strong trees felled in their prime.
Yellow headlights, gleaming wire wheels, gas pedal
to the floor. And on the windshield
painted in silver letters: *Learning to Fly.*

I'd have dressed you in tux, fancy lace shirt,
diamonds on the soles of your shoes —
a man can't go barefoot to Heaven.
Under the hood, I'd have laid you
in a cloud of pink clematis,
like those that bloomed the day you died.

Out of My Mind

1

My mind is littered with ghosts who
turn up uninvited. They revolve
on a stage with the corpse that clings
to my side. In shabby masks,
the same stilted actors come and go and
whisper wooden lines. My windows
are façades; my doors are bricked in.
Staircases end in mid-air.

2

I want a new dwelling
with no devils under the bed. I want
carpets of blossoms when the wind blows,
stairways awash with warm rain.
Waves that sculpt the shores
of my sleep. The hullabaloo
of wild turkeys at dawn. And nearby,
a little girl who leaves hibiscus at my door,
and asks if old ladies
become mermaids when they die.

Crossing Over

Last year, we came to this wild place
you used to love. Beside us, you plodded.
Vacant like a barnacle
whose soft insides have been pierced
and sucked clean by a gull.

Today, your father and I walk across
the sand bar again. Kelp that was swaying
hours ago in the deep, is flung now
across the beach like dishevelled hair.
Fish have retreated, blank-eyed,
but they will return, unaware of our passing.

There is a scud of fog, a shudder
of foghorns. Dampness clothes
our bones. We hug.
Silent houses on shore huddle
behind firs, branches ripped off by the wind.

Suddenly, sticky fog unclings. Clear sky
gleams, and the ocean parts, and there is sun
and warmth and joy. Yes, joy breaks through,
and there you are, there between us again,
for a moment as we cross over.

Sea Stars

They found the body of the drowned fisherman
in the Bay of Fundy. A starfish was clamped
on his face.

  • *Saint John Telegraph Journal*

Slow tentacles wave like explorers
departing on dangerous voyages.
They lose limbs, die marooned in the sun,
fly half-digested in a seagull beak.
Bat star, Cookie star, Mud star.

Leather star smelling of garlic.
Basket star — *Gorgoncephalus* —
engulfs prey three thousand feet down.
Fish-eating star consumes all
that lands on its spines. Blood, Vermillion.

Sunflower star straddles
with twenty-four arms. Fragile star
devours with five pulsing mouths.
Stars entangle below slurping tidelines
or sway in warm sea lettuce pools.

Braids of snakes. Coats of mail.
They cleave in sluggish clumps —
leather bodies with heavens on their backs.
Rainbow. Morning sunstar.
Amputated, they are born again from a ray.

Nine Months Dead

I dwell on you, your remains, sealed darkly
in a grey marble jar, a rose incised on the lid.
I cannot bury you. You are sorrow
that will not be contained, nor decanted in drops.

Nor can I bear to bring you home, set you
in honour on the mantel where parents display
their children, grandchildren.
This is *Randall, our Beloved Son,*
bits of bone and white ash in a stoppered urn.

Once I have clasped your small weight to my breast,
tell me, how am I to discard you?

Pegasus

Vex not his ghost: O! let him pass; he hates him
That would upon the rack of this tough world
Stretch him out longer.

•Shakespeare, *King Lear*

I no longer share your soul-skin
in demon-haunted streets; yet,
that was easier than this shearing-off, this writhing
Medusa of grief, these claws of bronze
and eyes that petrify. From that bloody head,

you sprang unshackled, white wings
shimmering in the streaking sky.
The ransom was your gain, not mine.
I sit on the stoney mountain, a nest
of nightmares in my lap. I mouth

the dry rustling of scales, the poor speech
of reptiles longing for incarnations —
I loved all of yours. Still, now,
I would play the greedy god,
and with a golden bridle, rein you in again.

The Grateful Dead

In Maryland, a young couple abandoned
their baby in a supermarket, took off to hear
a concert of *The Grateful Dead*.
That week, in her journal, the mother wrote
how alive she felt. In the hard rock land of Deadheads,
she had blotted the baby out.

I know the Judas mother. When strangers ask,
How many children? I deny you.
By omission. You are the pause
before the words of stone, *Only one.*
In the half-lie, you are the unsaid, the undead.
And I, the hermit crab, scuttle away,
drawing extremities behind me
into an imaginary womb
where I yearn to start life all over again.

In my dreams, stick figures flail and shout,
Ladybird, ladybird, fly away home,
your house is on fire, your children are gone.
I count and recount,
but you are always missing. I recite you
from shadows, *This is how he looked,*
and this is how he was. I resurrect images.
You are twelve in Aunt Mary's kitchen,
an adorable devil, singing
"Fifty Ways to Lose a Lover".

But there are days when I long to discard you
in a grocery cart, and walk away without a word,
pretending I am grateful you are dead.

Dreamscape

There, rooted in earth and death you lie,
your head shaven, your lean body pared down

to essentials. You weep for the
son, husband, father you might have been,

before you were landlocked with the dead.
Tears create their own barren landscape —

sinter and ashes and strangled plants,
the broken hoofprints of curious animals

who cannot drink the sulphurous brew.
Hissing geysers claw the sky, fall back again.

Lakes seethe under a steaming pall;
mountains roar in the night. In this wasteland,

I wipe away your tears, wait for your words.
At last you say, *Enough*. And from my heart,

burning lava flows in a long slow sweep
across and beyond, where no boundaries are.

Origami

Today, from a tangled Medusa head of
brittle seaweed, I gather crabs and
place them in the bowl of my new straw hat,
decorated with moss green ribbons and
peach silk rosebuds. Funeral bouquets for
tiny origami warriors in weightless armour
who rattle like dead leaves in a coffin and
shatter at my touch into a dessicated soup of
rigid pincers and claws, speckled carapaces and
little moonstone eyes on stalks that rotate but
do not see, and vanish when I squeeze them.

Only the shape of their scurrying remains and
the rank salty smell of their exquisite decay.

The Burial

Dew evaporates
And all our world is dew
So dear, so refreshing, so fleeting
•Issa

1

Two years we waited for the right moment.
Ritual. Words. But all that came was dread.
In the end, you included him
on your list of errands when you went to town:
go to the butcher
go to the bank
buy bread and salmon
pick up Randall's ashes.

2

While you were gone, I cleaned away
the oak leaves. It was time—
apple blossoms were springing from butchered limbs;
dogwood chalices brimmed with dew.

The leaves were sere—burnished leather
fingers entwined in corners,
reaching out of cracks in the deck.
I retrieved them one by one. Each mattered.

So many leaves I finally gave up on ceremony,
stuffed them by handfuls into a basket,
scattered them over the cliff
where winter's deadfall decays into spring.

3

Out of my sight, you poured the ashes
into a blue and white Chinese jar, covered them
with a lid—like funerary urns of old bones
we used to see in the hills of Hong Kong.

Easier to empty, you said, but you meant
quicker. We stumbled over seawrack and rocks
down to the shore. The sea was a-canter
and wild, our poor words drenched by waves.

You turned aside—*so the ashes don't blow in our faces.*
Is that what you meant? Afterwards, I wiped
around the inside of the jar, coated my fingertips
with the last of his fine dark dust.

The Rehearsal

I have written a mystery of youth,
destroyed by a hand that leaves no clues.
The plot is disorderly—a jigsaw no one solves—
and for the life of me, I cannot write the end.
His remains are sealed in a grey
marble urn. His mother cannot

dispose of the flesh of her flesh.
One day, one windy day (she promises herself)
when a brassy new sky is slashed by gulls,
and the sea gallops in—proud manes
humbled in froth on the rocks—
she will gather him up, amazed at this

last incongruous embrace, and she will
sleep-walk down to the shore, past the purple
shrouds of rockcress that cling to the walls,
and there on barnacle rocks,
she may behold him again as he
dives unafraid into the sea.

Holy Doors

Teach me the way and open the holy doors wide. . .
       • *The Aeneid*

I come home in spring—the bitter season
of your dying. The last trace
of winter's ordeal—a residue of salt
on the window, deadfall on the lawn.

On this point of land where you carved out
your pain, the pregnant earth
is longing again. You have slipped from me

through holy doors—your embrace
less fierce now. A slack tide lingers wistfully
in the cove, expectant like still morning.

In lacunas of time, I look for your radiance
in the haloes of clouds. I listen
for your voice in the towhee's song.

Notes

p. 61 In China, a young woman who dies young is called "queen of the night".

p. 65 Rose quartz is for the heart chakra, for giving and receiving love. It will dissolve all burdens and traumas that have hardened the heart.

p. 75 *Nakusp* from an Okanagan word meaning *closed in* or *come together.*

About the Author

Margo Button (*nee* Bartlett) was born in St. Andrews, New Brunswick. She has an Honours B.A. from the University of Toronto and an M.A. in French Literature from U.B.C. She taught high school in Ottawa for six years and at American international schools in Hong Kong, Lebanon and Chile. She has published widely in Canadian small magazines. This is her first book.

Margo Button lives with her husband in Nanoose Bay, B.C. and Puerto Vallarta, Mexico.